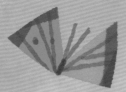

For best friends everywhere.
—J.R.

To Jeff, in our book that's made for two!
—J.C.

ME AND YOU IN A BOOK MADE FOR TWO

By Jean Reidy
Pictures by Joey Chou

HARPER
An Imprint of HarperCollinsPublishers

HOOOO!

Who?
Me and you!
You and me?
What would we do?

Life's an adventure—
a story—
that's true!

Now imagine our tale
in a book made for two!

What would we do in a book,
ME AND YOU?

Would we dance in a rainstorm
and dodge every drop?

Would we race on a rainbow
and meet at the top?

Would we repaint the world
and the universe too?

Would we seesaw on stars
while we take in the view?

From upside or downside—
WOW!—
life looks brand-new
in our brilliant and beautiful
book made for two.

Would we paddle the oceans?

Or pedal the land?

Play tag with twin crabs?
Tic-tac-toe in the sand?

Would we leapfrog
to lunch at a toad's
taco stand?

Play Ping-Pong with puffins,
completely unplanned?

Would we sing a duet with a jellyfish band—
A jellyfish band?
A jellyfish band!

Or an octopus orchestra.
That would be grand!

We might reach
twice as high.

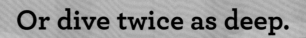
Or dive twice as deep.

We might share all our dreams
and the secrets we keep.

You would listen to me
and I'd listen to you.

We might see eye to eye
or a new point of view.

Would we write one long tale,
or a treasure of two,
sharing pages we'll bring to this book
made for two?

We might open our hearts
like we'd open a door.

We might lend a helping hand . . .
make that four.

With double the muscle
we're stronger than one.

Let's get this work started.
There's much to be done!

I'll push.
You'll pull.

We'll see this job through
in the fun we'll bring to this book,
me and you.

We might meet a friend.
We might make a friend. Yes!

We'll welcome new friends in our book, me and you.

Maybe one!
How about two?
Here comes three!
Yippee, four!
Why stop there?
We'll make room.

Welcome so many more!
So many friends—
WE'LL HAVE STORIES GALORE!!!

But before . . .

If a book about you
is a tale without end,
imagine what you might
do with a friend.

Here we go!

Take my hand!

Turn a page
or two.

What would we do in a book,
ME AND YOU?